Too Many

Written by Margaret Beames   Illustrated by Martyn van der Voo

Mr and Mrs Potts lived on a hill.
They lived in a lovely house
with steps down to the road.
There were twenty-seven steps down and
twenty-seven steps up again.

"This is a lovely house," they said,
"but oh dear, the steps!"

Every morning, Mrs Potts went down the steps
to get the milk –
twenty-seven steps down
and
twenty-seven steps up again.

Every lunchtime, Mr Potts went down the steps to get the letters –
twenty-seven steps down
and
twenty-seven steps up again.

Every afternoon, Mrs Potts went shopping –
twenty-seven steps down
and
twenty-seven steps up again.

Every evening, Mr Potts went down to get the newspaper –
twenty-seven steps down
and
twenty-seven steps up again.

"Too many steps," puffed Mr Potts.
"We will have to move."

"Far too many steps," puffed Mrs Potts.
"We will have to move."

Then they both said,
"But this is such a lovely house!"

Mr Potts had an idea.
He set right to work.

"What are you making?" asked Mrs Potts.

"Wait and see," said Mr Potts.

He worked all day.

"What are you making?" asked Mrs Potts again.

"Come and see," he said at last.

"Turn the wheel," said Mr Potts.

Mrs Potts turned the wheel.
A box came up on the end of the rope.
She turned the wheel again
and the box went down
on the end of the rope.

Every morning, Mrs Potts pulled up the box and there was the milk.

Every lunchtime, Mr Potts pulled up the box and there were the letters.

Every evening, Mr Potts pulled up the box and there was the newspaper.

But Mrs Potts still had to go shopping —
twenty-seven steps down
and
twenty-seven steps up again.

"Too many steps," she puffed.
Then Mrs Potts had an idea.
She sat in the box.
"Pull me up," she called.

Mr Potts began to turn the wheel
but Mrs Potts was too heavy.
The box began to creak. The wheel
began to squeak.

"Pull!" called Mrs Potts,
but it was no good.
The box began to slip
back down the steps.

It went faster and faster until
Bump! It hit the bottom.
Out fell Mrs Potts.
Out fell the shopping.
"Oh dear," said Mrs Potts
as she got up.

"Oh dear," she puffed
as she climbed up the steps.
"Twenty-seven steps down
and
twenty-seven steps up again.
Too many steps!"